First Facts™

Exploring the Animal Kingdom

Mammals

African elephants

by Adele Richardson

Consultant:
Robert T. Mason
Professor of Zoology, J. C. Braly Curator of Vertebrates
Oregon State University
Corvallis, Oregon

Capstone
press

Mankato, Minnesota

First Facts is published by Capstone Press
151 Good Counsel Drive, P.O. Box 669, Mankato, Minnesota 56002
www.capstonepress.com

Library of Congress Cataloging-in-Publication Data
Richardson, Adele, 1966–
    Mammals / by Adele Richardson
    p. cm.—(First facts. Exploring the animal kingdom)
    Includes bibliographical references (p. 23).
    ISBN 0-7368-2624-6 (hardcover)
    1. Mammals—Juvenile literature. [1. Mammals.] I. Title. II. Series.
QL706.2.R524 2005
599—dc22   2003026784

Summary: Discusses the characteristics, eating habits, and offspring of mammals, one of the main groups in the animal kingdom.

Editorial credits
Erika L. Shores, editor; Linda Clavel, designer; Kelly Garvin, photo researcher;
    Eric Kudalis, product planning editor

Photo credits
Ann & Rob Simpson, 17
Brand X Pictures/Guido Alberto Rossi, 1; John Lambert, 11 (top left)
Bruce Coleman Inc./Bruce Clendenning, 16; John Giustina, 18; L. Jane Ringe, 6–7
Corel, 11 (top right)
Creatas, cover (top left, main right), 9, 19
Dave Watts/naturepl.com, 20
DigitalVision/Gerry Ellis & Karl Ammann, cover (bottom left)
McDonald Wildlife Photography, cover (middle left), 11 (bottom left)
Minden Pictures/Thomas Mangelsen, 12–13; Konrad Wothe, 15
Photodisc/Teri Dixon, 11 (bottom right)

1 2 3 4 5 6 09 08 07 06 05 04

Table of Contents

Mammals

Mammals belong to the animal kingdom. People, dogs, and whales are mammals.

Other groups of animals live on land and in water with mammals. Birds have feathers. Reptiles have hard, dry skin. Amphibians have moist skin. Fish have fins. Insects have six legs.

Birds

Mammals

Reptiles

Main Animal Groups

Insects

Amphibians

Fish

Mammals Are Vertebrates

Mammals have backbones. Animals with backbones are called **vertebrates**. The backbone is part of an animal's **skeleton**. Muscles are joined to the skeleton. Muscles help this rabbit run, jump, and hop.

Fun Fact!
Adult mammals have skeletons made up of about 200 bones.

blacktail jackrabbit

7

Mammals Are Warm-Blooded

Mammals are warm-blooded. Their body temperatures stay the same in hot and cold weather.

Polar bears and other mammals turn food into **energy**. Their bodies use the energy to keep warm.

Fun Fact!
Polar bears have a thick layer of fat under their fur. The fat helps keep polar bears warm.

polar bear

Bodies of Mammals

Mammals can have legs, **flippers**, or wings. Most mammals have tails. Zebras walk on four legs. Dolphins and whales use their flippers to swim. Bats flap their wings to fly. Dogs run on four legs and wag their tails.

zebra

spinner dolphins

brown bat

dog

11

arctic fox

Mammals Have Hair

Mammals have hair on their bodies. Hair helps keep mammals warm. Most mammals have hair color that blends in with their surroundings. An arctic fox's white fur matches the snow and ice. It hides from **predators**.

Fun Fact!
In winter, the arctic fox has white fur. In spring, the fox's fur turns brown or gray.

How Mammals Breathe

Mammals breathe air with two **lungs**. Most mammals take in air for their lungs through their mouth or nose. Whales and dolphins breathe through blowholes on top of their heads.

killer whale

white-tailed deer

What Mammals Eat

Mammals eat plants, meat, or both.
Teeth help them chew, bite, or tear food.
Deer eat plants. They chew on leaves
with their flat teeth.

lions

Mammals with sharp teeth eat meat.
Lions catch **prey** with their sharp teeth.
People and raccoons have both sharp and
flat teeth for chewing and tearing food.

17

chimpanzees

Young Mammals

Most female mammals give birth to live young. The young drink milk made by their mothers. Chimpanzees and most other mammals care for their young.

Often, young mammals stay near their parents. Tiger cubs stay with their parents for about two years. Their mother teaches them to hunt.

bengal tigers

Amazing but True!

The platypus is an unusual mammal that lives only in Australia. A platypus has a flat bill like a duck. It also has webbed feet to help it swim. Unlike other mammals, a platypus lays eggs instead of giving birth to live young.

Compare the Main Animal Groups

	Vertebrates	Invertebrates	Warm-blooded	Cold-blooded	Hair	Feathers	Scales
Mammals	X		X		X		
Amphibians	X			X			
Birds	X		X			X	
Fish	X			X			X
Insects		X		X			
Reptiles	X			X			X

Glossary

energy (EN-ur-jee)—the ability to do work; a mammal uses food energy to keep its body warm.

flipper (FLIP-ur)—the armlike body part on the sides of a dolphin or a whale

lungs (LUHNGS)—organs inside the chest that animals use to breathe; air goes in and out of the lungs when animals breathe.

predator (PRED-uh-tur)—an animal that hunts other animals for food

prey (PRAY)—an animal that is hunted for food

skeleton (SKEL-uh-tuhn)—the bones that support and protect the body

vertebrate (VUR-tuh-bruht)—an animal that has a backbone

Read More

McEvoy, Paul. *Mammals.* Animal Facts. Philadelphia: Chelsea Clubhouse Books, 2003.

Unwin, Mike. *The Life Cycle of Mammals.* From Egg to Adult. Chicago: Heinemann Library, 2003.

Internet Sites

FactHound offers a safe, fun way to find Internet sites related to this book. All of the sites on FactHound have been researched by our staff.

Here's how:
1. Visit *www.facthound.com*
2. Type in this special code **0736826246** for age-appropriate sites. Or enter a search word related to this book for a more general search.
3. Click on the **Fetch It** button.

FactHound will fetch the best sites for you!

Index